For Caroline, Isaiah, Estlin, and Sir Gawain
—M.D.U.

Although I have known sorrow and great sadness,
as is everybody's lot, I do not think that I have
had an unhappy hour as a philosopher . . . I have
worked hard, and I have often got deep into
insoluble difficulties. But I have been most happy
in finding new problems, in wrestling with them,
and in making some progress. This, or so I feel,
is the best life.
   —Karl Popper (1902–1994), *Unended Quest*

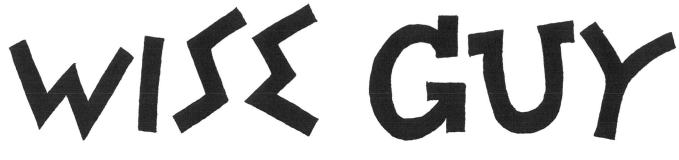

WISE GUY

The Life and Philosophy of Socrates

M. D. Usher
Pictures by William Bramhall

Farrar Straus Giroux
New York

Long ago in ancient Greece, a boy named Socrates declared that all he knew was nothing. So he spent his whole life asking questions.

He was a curious boy, and cheeky too, but more than anything in all the world he wanted to be happy, he wanted to be good, and he wanted to be *wise*.

Socrates lived in the city-state of Athens from 469 to 399 B.C.E. All his life he loved to ask mind-boggling questions. Take, for example, his most famous remark, "I know that I know nothing." This cannot be completely true, if you think about it. Anyone who says such a thing knows at least *one* thing: that he knows nothing. And of course that same person knows many other things as well, like how to walk, talk, or eat. What Socrates meant is that you shouldn't think you know something without having first looked at it very closely. He believed that asking good questions was far more interesting and important than having all the answers because, little by little, this would lead to a better understanding of things, and understanding is the beginning of wisdom. In a world full of know-it-alls, Socrates was brave enough to admit his ignorance. In fact, he never claimed to possess the knowledge he sought, and though he had many followers, he did not let anyone call him a teacher.

Every day he went to see his friend, a cobbler named Simon. He sat and studied Simon while he worked. Simon cut leather into strips and stitched the pieces carefully together into shoes. He was an excellent cobbler.

"Hmmm," Socrates wondered. "Is cobbling a kind of wisdom?"

Simon the Cobbler is said to have been the first person to write what are known as *Socratic dialogues*, which were probably based on actual conversations between Socrates and other men. (Socrates himself wrote nothing.) A more famous follower of Socrates named Plato (429–347 B.C.E.) perfected this style of writing, and his dialogues are classics of world literature that have been read by all sorts of people for over two thousand years.

Socrates was very much at home with working-class people like Simon. He himself was the son of a stonemason and probably worked in that trade as a young man. When discussing things, Socrates liked to take examples from the world of craftsmen and laborers. This annoyed some of his friends and fellow citizens. A rich politician named Callicles (KAL-ih-kleez) once complained, "Good god, Socrates, you just go on and on about cobblers, washerwomen, and cooks, don't you, as if they had something to do with the argument!" But Socrates was convinced they had *everything* to do with his arguments. He believed wisdom was an art, like cobbling, that you have to practice if you're going to be any good at it.

He also watched a carpenter in town build furniture from wood. First the carpenter built a bed, then he built a table, each as finely crafted as the other.

"Hmmm," Socrates pondered. "If both are made of wood and have four legs, what makes one a table and one a bed? And what makes a carpenter a carpenter?" Socrates scratched his head. "It must have something to do with *ideas*," he decided.

What is an idea? Is it a thing you can smell, taste, or touch? If not, is it any less real than a bed or table? What is the difference between the *idea* of a bed and the bed itself? Socrates argued that the carpenter must have an idea or image of a bed in his mind before he can go about building one. But where does this idea come from in the first place? Socrates seems to have believed that objects in our world have an invisible, eternal blueprint to which they correspond. The eternal blueprint of a bed may not seem so very interesting, but Socrates applied the idea to larger concepts, like right and wrong and good and bad. Just as a carpenter with vast knowledge and experience can make a good bed, and in turn be a good carpenter, a person who has studied the blueprint of right and wrong can be a good person.

He thought a lot about ideas, and questioned everyone to find out more:
"What about ideas you cannot see as you would a table or a bed?
"What is *goodness*? What is *courage*? What is *justice*? What is *love*?"
Though important people huffed and puffed, claiming to know the answers and pretending to be wise, he found that no one understood ideas as Simon understood his leather, or the carpenter his wood.
"How can you be truly wise if you don't know what these things are?" Socrates asked.

Socrates once said that, based on his experience, the people with the best reputations tend to be the ones who know the least. The reason for this, he thought, was that people who are overly concerned about how they look or *seem* to others fail to see themselves for who and what they really *are*. In other words, the more time and energy someone spends on *looking* good, the less good he or she will actually *be*.

Because he believed that things are not always what they seem, Socrates questioned the simple words we take for granted—like "goodness," "courage," "justice," or "love." He wanted to strip away any false assumptions we make in constructing ideas such as these, and build up a new, more precise definition from scratch. He called this process *dialectic* (DYE-uh-LEK-tik), which is a Greek word for an intense, logical conversation. Dialectic, according to Socrates, is what philosophy is all about.

People listened closely to his questions. They'd sit outside for hours in the warm, inviting sun.

"Hmmm," Socrates said, looking up into the sky. "Do you think goodness might be like the sun, the source of vision, light, and life?"

We rely upon the sun in order to see and live. Just as life is impossible without it, says Socrates, so we cannot live without goodness. But the sun does not shine everywhere on everyone all the time. Likewise, people tend not to be good all the time.

Socrates' admirer Plato compared people without knowledge to prisoners who spend their entire lives in a cave. There they sit, chained with their backs to a high wall in such a way that they can't turn their heads around. Above and behind them, at the entrance to the cave, people and objects pass by in the light of the sun, casting faint shadows on the wall in front of the prisoners deep within. But because they have never seen anything in the direct light of the sun, the prisoners only know the shadows; they have no idea what the things casting the shadows look like. They argue about the meaning of the shadows, and are so sure of themselves that even when someone climbs into the cave and tells them that what they see are only shadows, most of the prisoners don't believe it. The few who are willing to accept that they may be wrong can escape from the cave, but they must proceed carefully and slowly in order to let their eyes adjust to the light. For Plato, Socrates was like a man trying to free cave dwellers who are chained to their own way of thinking.

And when the sun went down, as it always does, Socrates would spend the night with friends. They'd eat and drink and talk . . .

. . . and DANCE! Socrates loved to dance and wave his arms and twist his hips.

"The body, like the mind," he said, "must be nimble, fit, and strong."

The Greeks loved parties, and their philosophers were no exception. Even as an old man, Socrates was popular among young people, and would entertain them late into the night with his conversation. He could out-think and out-talk anybody. Sometimes, when everyone else had gone to sleep, he would stay up all night thinking through a problem.

Socrates was famous for his physical toughness too. He never wore shoes, even when serving in the army in northern Greece, where he amazed his fellow soldiers by marching barefoot through snow without a complaint. On at least two occasions he fought bravely in battle and once risked his life to save a young friend named Alcibiades (AL-sih-BYE-uh-deez). But in spite of his bravery and his incredible powers of concentration, Socrates did not take himself too seriously. He knew how to enjoy himself as well.

But he was not a very handsome man. Some people ridiculed the way he looked—part crab, part pig, part donkey.

He didn't mind their jokes. He just smiled and said, "I see better with these bulging eyes, smell better with my turned-up nose, kiss better with these donkey lips!"

The Greeks were great lovers of beauty. They prized young, thin, athletic bodies, and Socrates did not fit into their classical ideal. One of Socrates' most passionate followers, the handsome, swashbuckling Alcibiades, once compared him to a smelly, goatlike creature called a satyr (SAY-tur). Still, Alcibiades confessed, he found Socrates irresistible: Socrates' words, he said, were like the magic of the pipe-playing satyr Marsyas (MAHR-see-us) from Greek myth, who could charm the whole world with his song, despite his appearance.

Socrates was also poor, but happy with the things he had.

"Look at all the things I do not need!" he'd say with a laugh whenever he went shopping.

Since the future is always uncertain and often out of our control, Socrates believed that we should prize most highly those things that cannot be taken away from us, no matter what happens—good thoughts and a correct attitude toward life. He tried to convince people not to look for happiness in wealth or fame. Rather, he argued, it is the person who wants what good things he or she already has who is the happiest of all.

And when he prayed, which he sometimes did, his prayer went like this:

Dear Pan, and all you gods here, graciously
    Grant that I be beautiful within,
And may my behavior in this world agree
    With what is hidden underneath this skin.
And may I count the wise man rich,
    And desire only so much gold
As the modest purse of a prudent man
    Would want to have or hold.

This prayer to the god of woods and pastures is spoken by Socrates at the end of Plato's dialogue the *Phaedrus* (FEE-drus). Though he was often critical of the gods of Greek mythology—especially of all their lying, stealing, fighting, and cheating— Socrates was a deeply religious man. Ever since his boyhood, he tells us, he had a special guardian spirit watching over him. The spirit would never tell him what to do (he had to think *that* through for himself), but he claimed it would warn him with a divine sign when he was about to do or encounter something bad.

Apollo, god of wisdom, loved Socrates dearly. "No one is as wise, or good, or brave as he," Apollo said.

The other gods agreed.

Socrates had an admiring friend named Chaerephon (KY-ruh-fon), who was puzzled by Socrates and his claim to know nothing. Chaerephon decided to travel to the town of Delphi (DEL-fee) in order to ask the god Apollo who, if not Socrates, was the wisest man in the world. The temple of Apollo there was home to a priestess called the Pythia (PIH-thee-uh), who would answer people's questions by divine inspiration from Apollo. Her answer to Chaerephon is reported to have been this:

> Sophocles is smart, Euripides
> is smarter,
> But smartest of the smartest lot
> is Socrates!

Sophocles (SAW-fuh-kleez) and Euripides (yoo-RIH-puh-deez) were brilliant and successful dramatists—two of the most famous poets in Greece at that time. When Socrates heard Apollo's answer, he concluded that the only way he could be considered the wisest man of all was because he alone of all men knew that he knew nothing. Encouraged by Apollo's response, Socrates began to view his life in philosophy as a kind of religious service—especially because he didn't get paid for it like most teachers of his day. He even joked to his fellow Athenians that he'd been sent to them from the gods like a pesky gadfly who stings a sleeping horse into a full gallop.

But certain men were not so pleased. "How can a man who says that he knows nothing be the wisest man of all?" they grumbled.

They felt threatened. They were jealous and embarrassed.

So they accused the thinker Socrates of things he never did or said. Then they sent him off . . .

. . . to *jail*!

Socrates was sad. "Nevertheless," he said, "it is still better
to suffer a wrong than to commit one."

Socrates was charged with corrupting the youth and not believing in the city's gods. These, however, were false charges; it was really his free manner of speaking that got him into trouble. In the end, after a trial at which he gave a speech, Socrates was condemned to death by a narrow margin. The law allowed him to plead for a more lenient sentence, but Socrates refused to do so. Instead, he proposed that, like a victorious Olympic athlete, he should be housed and fed at the city's expense because of the service he had performed all his life in trying to make himself and his fellow citizens better people. This infuriated the court and only confirmed his death sentence. Socrates wasn't scared of death, however, because he believed that goodness is its own reward and that nothing truly bad can happen to a good person.

His friends came every day to visit him in jail. They talked—and DANCED!—until he died.

"Friends," he used to say, "have things in common."

Socrates was sentenced to drink poison hemlock, but this was delayed because, by law, no executions could be performed until a sacred ship had returned from the island of Delos (DEE-loss). This gave Socrates a few extra days to spend with family and friends. While in prison, he passed the time discussing ideas as usual, and he set some of the fables of Aesop (EE-sop) to music. One of Socrates' wealthy friends, Crito (KRY-toh), made arrangements for his escape, but Socrates refused to leave the jail, arguing that someone who enjoys the rights and privileges of the rule of law must also accept the verdicts issued by the law—even if the law is wrong. In such cases, he insisted, citizens and lawmakers should be peacefully persuaded to change unjust laws. Socrates was seventy years old when he died.

The saying "Friends have things in common" is an old proverb the Greeks traced back to Pythagoras (pih-THA-goh-rus), a musician and mathematician who was the first person to call himself a philosopher, which is a Greek word meaning "friend of wisdom." Socrates' way of life has inspired countless people throughout history, some of whom are pictured here.

And his friends have been asking questions ever since.

Socrates' "School of Athens"

Desiderius Erasmus (DEH-zih-DAIR-ee-us ih-RAZ-mus, 1466–1536)
Dutch scholar and humanist

Erasmus was one of the few men of his time who could read classical Greek. He called Socrates "the epitome of a true philosopher. He despised all those things for which other mortals strive and sail the seas, sweat, and go to court, even go to war. He was untouched by insults, and neither good fortune nor bad had any impact on him. He feared nothing, not even death, which scares everybody."

From an essay entitled "The Sileni of Alcibiades," quoted here from Utopia *by Thomas More, with Erasmus's The Sileni of Alcibiades, translated by David Wootton (Indianapolis: Hackett, 1999), p. 170.*

Thomas Jefferson (1743–1826)
American president, architect, farmer, and amateur philosopher

Jefferson admired Socrates but, like many people before and since, thought that Plato had put too many of his own ideas into Socrates' mouth. In 1813 fellow statesman John Adams wrote to Jefferson, asking him what he thought about Socrates' guardian spirit. Jefferson replied: "[Socrates] was too wise to believe and too honest to pretend, that he had real and familiar converse with a superior and invisible being. He probably considered the suggestions of his conscience, or reason, as revelations or inspirations from the Supreme mind, bestowed, on important occasions, by a special superintending Providence."

From a letter written at Jefferson's home of Monticello to John Adams, dated October 12, 1813; quoted from The Writings of Thomas Jefferson, *volume 13, edited by Albert Ellery Bergh (Washington, D.C.: Thomas Jefferson Memorial Association, 1907), pp. 391–92.*

Søren Kierkegaard (SOHR-en KEER-kuh-gard, 1813–1855)
Danish philosopher and theologian

Kierkegaard expended a lot of mental energy trying to come to grips with Socrates' elusive personality: "Forming a conception of Socrates . . . is quite another matter than forming a conception of most other men . . . As there are now thousands of years between him and us, and since not even his contemporaries could grasp him . . . one easily sees how difficult it becomes to secure an image of him . . . It seems impossible, or at least as baffling as trying to depict an elf wearing a hat that makes him invisible."

From Kierkegaard's 1841 M.A. thesis, The Concept of Irony, with Constant Reference to Socrates, *translated by Lee M. Capel (London: Collins, 1966), p. 50.*

Friedrich Nietzsche (FREE-drik NEE-chuh, 1844–1900)
German philosopher and classical scholar

Nietzsche was highly critical of Socrates' logical approach to life, but he also recognized Socrates' less rational side, calling him "the buffoon who got himself taken seriously."

From Twilight of the Idols, *quoted from* The Portable Nietzsche, *edited and translated by Walter Kaufmann (London and New York: Penguin, 1954), p. 476.*

Mahatma Gandhi (ma-HAHT-ma GAHN-dee, 1869–1948)
Hindu political reformer of India, activist, and sage

Gandhi considered Socrates, whom he liked to call "Sukrit," a *satyagrahi*, or inspired seeker of truth. In response to a young student's question about the relationship between Beauty and Truth in art, Gandhi replied: "Socrates, we are told, was the most truthful man of his time and yet his features were said to have been the ugliest in Greece. To my mind he was beautiful, because all his life was a striving after Truth."

From a conversation recorded in 1924, quoted from The Moral and Political Writings of Mahatma Gandhi, *volume 2, edited by Raghavan Iyer (Oxford: Clarendon, 1986), p. 180.*

Bertrand Russell (1872–1970)
British philosopher, mathematician, and social activist

Russell was a master logician who tried to put logical thinking to work for the good of society. About the Socratic method he once wrote: "Logical errors are, I think, of greater practical importance than many people believe; they enable their perpetrators to hold the comfortable opinion on every subject in turn. Any logically coherent body of doctrine is sure to be in part painful and contrary to current prejudices. The dialectical method—or, more generally, the habit of unfettered discussion—tends to promote a logical consistency, and is in this way useful."

From Bertrand Russell, A History of Western Philosophy *(New York: Simon & Schuster, 1945), p. 93.*

Ludwig Wittgenstein (LOOD-vig VIT-gen-shtine, 1889–1951)
Austrian-born mechanical engineer turned philosopher

Wittgenstein was in many ways like Socrates in his lifelong quest for truth and in his claim never to have grasped it. Sometimes, however, he got frustrated: "Reading the Socratic dialogues one has the feeling: what a frightful waste of time! What's the point of these arguments that prove nothing and clarify nothing?"

An observation dated 1931, quoted from Culture and Value, *edited by G. H. von Wright, translated by Peter Winch (Oxford: Blackwell, 1980), p. 14.*

Hannah Arendt (HAH-nah ah-RENT, 1906–1975)
American political philosopher of German-Jewish descent

Arendt escaped from Nazi Germany to France in 1933, and then from occupied France to the United States in 1941. Her experiences led her to be sharply critical of repressive governments and elitist philosophies. She was a great admirer of Socrates, about whom she wrote: "None of [his] arguments ever stays put; they move around. And because Socrates, asking questions to which he does *not* know the answers, sets them in motion, once the statements have come full circle, it is usually Socrates who cheerfully proposes to start all over again and inquire what justice or piety or knowledge or happiness are. For the topics of [his] dialogues deal with very simple, everyday concepts, such as arise whenever people open their mouths and begin to talk."

From Hannah Arendt, The Life of the Mind, *volume 1:* Thinking *(New York: Harcourt Brace Jovanovich, 1978), pp. 169–70.*

Martin Luther King Jr. (1929–1968)
American civil rights leader and Baptist minister

In a famous letter written from a Birmingham, Alabama, jail in 1963, King found encouragement in the example of Socrates: "I am not afraid of the word 'tension.' I have earnestly opposed violent tension, but there is a type of constructive, nonviolent tension which is necessary for growth. Just as Socrates felt that it was necessary to create a tension in the mind so that individuals could rise from the bondage of myths and half-truths to the unfettered realm of creative analysis and objective appraisal, so must we see the need for nonviolent gadflies to create the kind of tension in society that will help men rise from the dark depths of prejudice and racism to the majestic heights of understanding and brotherhood."

From Martin Luther King Jr., Why We Can't Wait *(New York: Harper & Row, 1964), p. 81.*

The Ancient Sources

This book is based entirely on ancient sources, with one exception: Socrates' adult interests have been imaginatively read back into his youth. In point of fact, we know very little about Socrates' childhood. It is as if he springs full-grown from the heads of Plato, Xenophon (ZEH-nuh-fon), and the other ancient authors who wrote about him. We do know, however, that he believed it is never too early to start thinking philosophically: "Someone who loves learning," he says in Plato's *Republic* (495d), "must strive for every kind of truth from childhood on."

The following is not an exhaustive list of all ancient sources that deal with the detail or issue in question, but it does indicate the main sources on which a given choice of text in this book is based. Note: The numbers by which Platonic dialogues are cited are called Stephanus numbers. They represent the page, section, and line numbers of an important Greek edition of Plato's works published by Henri Etienne ("Stephanus") in 1578. Translations of all of Plato's dialogues are conveniently collected in *Plato: Complete Works*, edited, with introduction and notes, by John M. Cooper and D. S. Hutchinson (Indianapolis: Hackett, 1997).

The slogan "I know that I know nothing" comes from Plato, *Apology* 21d. The claim never to have been a teacher is from *Apology* 33a.

For Simon the Cobbler, see Diogenes Laertius, *Lives of Eminent Philosophers* 2.122, who is also the source for the belief that Socrates was the son of a stonemason (2.18–19). The complaint about washerwomen and cooks comes from Plato, *Gorgias* 491a. For the idea of wisdom as an art, see *Gorgias* 458e–461b.

The classic discussion of ideas, beds, and tables is from Plato, *Republic* 595–598d.

Skepticism about good reputations is expressed in Plato, *Apology* 21c–22c9. The moral qualities listed on this page are the sorts of things Socrates habitually discussed: for goodness, see Plato, *Republic* 504–511e; for courage, see Plato's *Laches*; for justice, see in particular *Republic*, Book 1; on love, see Plato's *Symposium* and *Lysis*.

The sun analogy appears in Plato, *Republic* 507–509d; the cave, in *Republic* 514–532e.

On Socratic dancing, see Xenophon, *Symposium* 2.10. On the importance of strong bodies and minds, see Plato, *Republic* 403c–410a. Socrates' physical and mental toughness and bravery are celebrated in Plato, *Symposium* 219d–221c and *Apology* 28d–e.

On Socrates' face, see Xenophon, *Symposium* 5–6. For Socrates as a satyr, see Plato, *Symposium* 215a–216e.

On Socrates' poverty, see Plato, *Apology* 4.12–13. The "things I do not need" anecdote is taken from Diogenes Laertius, *Lives of Eminent Philosophers* 2.25.

The prayer to Pan is taken from Plato, *Phaedrus* 279b–c. For Socrates' divine sign, see Plato, *Apology* 31d–32d9, Xenophon, *Memorabilia* 1.1.29, and Xenophon, *Apology* 4.12–13.

For Chaerephon's visit to the oracle of Apollo, see Plato, *Apology* 20e–23c. The Pythia's response (probably spurious) comes from an ancient commentary on the *Apology* by Aretas, in *Scholia Platonica*, edited by William Chase Greene (Haverford, Pa.: American Philological Association, 1938), p. 422. On Socrates as a gadfly, see *Apology* 30e1–9.

The term "thinker" used in a derogatory way comes from Aristophanes, *Clouds* (see also Plato, *Apology* 18b). The doctrine that it is better to suffer a wrong than to commit one is found at Plato, *Gorgias* 479e. For the criminal charges, Socrates' counterproposal, and his fearlessness in the face of death, see *Apology* 19b–c and 36b–42a.

Details of Socrates' imprisonment (the poison, the sacred ship, Aesop's fables) are found in Plato's *Phaedo*. The debate about whether or not to escape from prison is from Plato's *Crito*.

For Further Reading

Thomas C. Brickhouse and Nicholas D. Smith, *The Philosophy of Socrates* (Boulder, Colo.: Westview Press, 2000).

Diskin Clay, *Platonic Questions: Dialogues with the Silent Philosopher* (University Park: Pennsylvania State University Press, 2000).

Karl Jaspers, *Socrates, Buddha, Confucius, Jesus: The Paradigmatic Individuals*, edited by Hannah Arendt, translated by Ralph Manheim (San Diego: Harcourt Brace Jovanovich, 1985).

Hope May, *On Socrates* (Belmont, Calif.: Wadsworth Publishing, 1999).

Alexander Nehamas, *Virtues of Authenticity: Essays on Plato and Socrates* (Princeton, N.J.: Princeton University Press, 1998).

R. B. Rutherford, *The Art of Plato: Ten Essays in Platonic Interpretation* (Cambridge, Mass.: Harvard University Press, 1995).

C. C. W. Taylor, *Socrates: A Very Short Introduction* (New York: Oxford University Press, 2000).

Gregory Vlastos, *Socrates: Ironist and Moral Philosopher* (Ithaca, N.Y.: Cornell University Press, 1991).